SOUND INNOVATIONS

ENSEMBLE DEVELOPMENT
Chorales and Warm-up Exercises for Tone, Technique and Rhythm
ADVANCED CONCERT BAND

Peter **BOONSHAFT** | Chris **BERNOTAS**

Thank you for making *Sound Innovations: Ensemble Development for Advanced Concert Band* a part of your concert band curriculum. With 399 exercises, including over 70 chorales by some of today's most renowned composers for concert band, it is our hope you will find this book to be a valuable resource in helping you grow in your understanding and abilities as an ensemble musician.

An assortment of exercises are grouped by key and presented in a variety of difficulty levels. Where possible, several exercises in the same category are provided to allow for variety while accomplishing the goals of that specific type of exercise. You will notice that many exercises and chorales are clearly marked with dynamics, articulations, style, and tempo for you to practice those aspects of performance. Other exercises are intentionally left for you or your teacher to determine how best to use them in reaching your performance goals.

Whether you are progressing through exercises to better your technical facility or to challenge your musicianship with beautiful chorales, we are confident you will be excited, motivated, and inspired by using *Sound Innovations: Ensemble Development for Advanced Concert Band.*

© 2014 Alfred Music
Sound Innovations™ is a trademark of Alfred Music
All Rights Reserved including Public Performance

ISBN-10: 1-4706-1814-1
ISBN-13: 978-1-4706-1814-8

Instrument photos courtesy of Yamaha Corporation of America Band & Orchestral Division

Concert B♭ Major

1 **PASSING THE TONIC**

2 **PASSING THE TONIC**

3 **PASSING THE TONIC**

4 **LONG TONES**

5 **LONG TONES**

6 **LONG TONES**

7 **CONCERT B♭ MAJOR SCALE**

8 **SCALE PATTERN**

9 SCALE PATTERN

10 CONCERT B♭ CHROMATIC SCALE

11 CHROMATIC SCALE PATTERN

12 FLEXIBILITY

13 FLEXIBILITY

14 FLEXIBILITY

15 CHROMATIC FLEXIBILITY

25 EXPANDING INTERVALS: DOWNWARD IN PARALLEL OCTAVES

26 EXPANDING INTERVALS: UPWARD IN PARALLEL FIFTHS

27 EXPANDING INTERVALS: DOWNWARD IN TRIADS

28 EXPANDING INTERVALS: UPWARD IN TRIADS

29 RHYTHM: SIMPLE METER (4/4)

30 RHYTHM: COMPOUND METER (6/8)

31 RHYTHMIC SUBDIVISION

32 CHANGING METER 6/8 AND 3/4

33 CHANGING METER 4/4 AND 5/8

(2+3)

34 CONCERT B♭ MAJOR SCALE AND CHORALE

Chris M. Bernotas (ASCAP)

35 CHORALE

Randall D. Standridge (ASCAP)

36 CHORALE

Rossano Galante

Andante

37 CHORALE

Jack Stamp

Pastorale

38 CHORALE

David R. Gillingham

Moderately, with expression

39 CHORALE

Andrew Boysen, Jr.

Slow and sweet

A tempo

Concert G Minor

47 PASSING THE TONIC

48 LONG TONES

49 CONCERT G NATURAL MINOR SCALE

50 CONCERT G HARMONIC AND MELODIC MINOR SCALES

51 SCALE PATTERN

52 SCALE PATTERN

53 FLEXIBILITY

54 CHROMATIC FLEXIBILITY

55 ARPEGGIOS

56 ARPEGGIOS

57 INTERVALS

58 INTERVALS

59 BALANCE AND INTONATION: DIATONIC HARMONY

60 BALANCE AND INTONATION: MOVING CHORD TONES

61 BALANCE AND INTONATION: LAYERED TUNING

62 BALANCE AND INTONATION: FAMILY BALANCE

63 EXPANDING INTERVALS: DOWNWARD IN PARALLEL OCTAVES

64 EXPANDING INTERVALS: DOWNWARD IN TRIADS

65 EXPANDING INTERVALS: UPWARD IN TRIADS

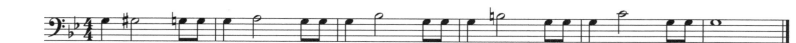

66 RHYTHM: SIMPLE METER ($\frac{4}{4}$)

67 RHYTHM: COMPOUND METER ($\frac{3}{8}$)

68 RHYTHMIC SUBDIVISION

69 CHANGING METER $\frac{3}{4}$ AND $\frac{6}{8}$

70 CONCERT G MINOR SCALE AND CHORALE

Chris M. Bernotas (ASCAP)

71 CHORALE

Rossano Galante

72 CHORALE

Jack Stamp

73 CHORALE

David R. Gillingham

74 CHORALE

Stephen Melillo (ASCAP)

75 CHORALE

Andrew Boysen, Jr.

12

Concert E♭ Major

76   **PASSING THE TONIC**

77   **PASSING THE TONIC**

78   **PASSING THE TONIC**

79   **LONG TONES**

80   **LONG TONES**

81   **LONG TONES**

82   **CONCERT E♭ MAJOR SCALE**

83   **SCALE PATTERN**

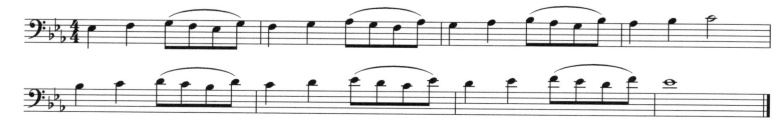

84 **SCALE PATTERN**

85 **CONCERT E♭ CHROMATIC SCALE**

86 **CHROMATIC SCALE PATTERN**

87 **FLEXIBILITY**

88 **FLEXIBILITY**

89 **FLEXIBILITY**

90 **CHROMATIC FLEXIBILITY**

91 ARPEGGIOS

92 ARPEGGIOS

93 INTERVALS

94 INTERVALS

95 BALANCE AND INTONATION: PERFECT INTERVALS

96 BALANCE AND INTONATION: DIATONIC HARMONY

97 BALANCE AND INTONATION: LAYERED TUNING

98 BALANCE AND INTONATION: MOVING CHORD TONES

99 BALANCE AND INTONATION: SHIFTING CHORD QUALITIES

100 EXPANDING INTERVALS: DOWNWARD IN PARALLEL OCTAVES

101 EXPANDING INTERVALS: DOWNWARD IN PARALLEL FIFTHS

102 EXPANDING INTERVALS: DOWNWARD IN TRIADS

103 EXPANDING INTERVALS: UPWARD IN TRIADS

104 RHYTHM: SIMPLE METER (4/4)

105 RHYTHM: COMPOUND METER (12/8)

106 RHYTHMIC SUBDIVISION

107 CHANGING METER 4/4 AND 3/8

108 CHANGING METER 3/4 AND 5/8

115 CHORALE: GOD IN THE HEAVENS AND IN THE EARTH

Johann Sebastian Bach (1685–1750)
Arranged by Todd Stalter

Lento

116 CHORALE

Robert Sheldon

With hope

A tempo

117 CHORALE

Andrew Boysen, Jr.

Stately and pompous

118 CHORALE

Stephen Melillo (ASCAP)

Rubato, slowly as felt

119 CHORALE

Jack Stamp

Flowing

120 CHORALE

David R. Gillingham

With grace

A tempo

Concert C Minor

121 PASSING THE TONIC

122 LONG TONES

123 CONCERT C NATURAL MINOR SCALE

124 CONCERT C HARMONIC AND MELODIC MINOR SCALES

125 SCALE PATTERN

126 SCALE PATTERN

127 FLEXIBILITY

128 CHROMATIC FLEXIBILITY

129 **ARPEGGIOS**

130 **ARPEGGIOS**

131 **INTERVALS**

132 **INTERVALS**

133 **BALANCE AND INTONATION: DIATONIC HARMONY**

134 **BALANCE AND INTONATION: MOVING CHORD TONES**

135 **BALANCE AND INTONATION: LAYERED TUNING**

136 **BALANCE AND INTONATION: FAMILY BALANCE**

137 EXPANDING INTERVALS: DOWNWARD IN PARALLEL OCTAVES

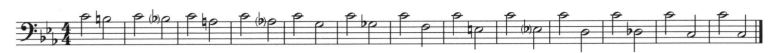

138 EXPANDING INTERVALS: DOWNWARD IN TRIADS

139 EXPANDING INTERVALS: UPWARD IN TRIADS

140 RHYTHM ($\frac{5}{4}$)

141 RHYTHM: COMPOUND METER ($\frac{6}{8}$)

142 RHYTHMIC SUBDIVISION

143 CHANGING METER: $\frac{4}{4}$ AND $\frac{7}{8}$

Concert F Major

150 PASSING THE TONIC

151 LONG TONES

152 CONCERT F MAJOR SCALE

153 CONCERT F CHROMATIC SCALE

154 SCALE PATTERN

155 SCALE PATTERN

156 FLEXIBILITY

157 CHROMATIC FLEXIBILITY

158 ARPEGGIOS

159 ARPEGGIOS

160 INTERVALS

161 INTERVALS

162 BALANCE AND INTONATION: DIATONIC HARMONY

163 BALANCE AND INTONATION: MOVING CHORD TONES

164 BALANCE AND INTONATION: LAYERED TUNING

165 BALANCE AND INTONATION: FAMILY BALANCE

166 **EXPANDING INTERVALS: DOWNWARD IN PARALLEL OCTAVES**

167 **EXPANDING INTERVALS: DOWNWARD IN TRIADS**

168 **EXPANDING INTERVALS: UPWARD IN TRIADS**

169 **RHYTHM: SIMPLE METER (4/4)**

170 **RHYTHM: COMPOUND METER (9/8)**

171 **RHYTHMIC SUBDIVISION**

172 **CHANGING METER: 4/4 AND 7/8**

(2+2+3)

Concert D Minor

179 **PASSING THE TONIC**

180 **LONG TONES**

181 **CONCERT D NATURAL MINOR SCALE**

182 **CONCERT D HARMONIC AND MELODIC MINOR SCALES**

183 **SCALE PATTERN**

184 **SCALE PATTERN**

185 **FLEXIBILITY**

186 **CHROMATIC FLEXIBILITY**

187 ARPEGGIOS

188 ARPEGGIOS

189 INTERVALS

190 INTERVALS

191 BALANCE AND INTONATION: DIATONIC HARMONY

192 BALANCE AND INTONATION: MOVING CHORD TONES

193 BALANCE AND INTONATION: LAYERED TUNING

194 BALANCE AND INTONATION: FAMILY BALANCE

195 **EXPANDING INTERVALS: DOWNWARD IN PARALLEL OCTAVES**

196 **EXPANDING INTERVALS: DOWNWARD IN TRIADS**

197 **EXPANDING INTERVALS: UPWARD IN TRIADS**

198 **RHYTHM (6/4)**

199 **RHYTHM: COMPOUND METER (6/8)**

200 **RHYTHMIC SUBDIVISION**

201 **CHANGING METER: 4/4 AND 7/8**

202 **CONCERT D MINOR SCALE AND CHORALE**

Chris M. Bernotas (ASCAP)

203 **CHORALE**

Robert Sheldon

Somber

204 **CHORALE**

Michael Story (ASCAP)

Andante

205 **CHORALE**

Chris M. Bernotas (ASCAP)

Andante

206 **CHORALE: PRÄLUDIUM**

Arcangelo Corelli (1653–1713)
Edited and Arranged by Todd Stalter

Adagio

207 **CHORALE**

Rossano Galante

Lento

Concert A♭ Major

208 **PASSING THE TONIC**

209 **LONG TONES**

210 **CONCERT A♭ MAJOR SCALE**

211 **SCALE PATTERN**

212 **SCALE PATTERN**

213 **CONCERT A♭ CHROMATIC SCALE**

214 **FLEXIBILITY**

215 **CHROMATIC FLEXIBILITY**

32

224 EXPANDING INTERVALS: DOWNWARD IN PARALLEL OCTAVES

225 EXPANDING INTERVALS: DOWNWARD IN TRIADS

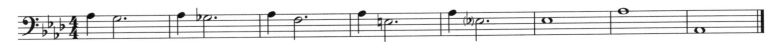

226 EXPANDING INTERVALS: UPWARD IN TRIADS

227 RHYTHM: SIMPLE METER ($\frac{4}{4}$)

228 RHYTHM: COMPOUND METER ($\frac{9}{8}$)

229 RHYTHMIC SUBDIVISION ($\frac{4}{4}$)

230 CHANGING METER: $\frac{4}{4}$ AND $\frac{6}{8}$ AND $\frac{3}{4}$

Concert F Minor

237 PASSING THE TONIC

238 LONG TONES

239 CONCERT F NATURAL MINOR SCALE

240 CONCERT F HARMONIC AND MELODIC MINOR SCALES

241 SCALE PATTERN

242 SCALE PATTERN

243 FLEXIBILITY

244 CHROMATIC FLEXIBILITY

245 ARPEGGIOS

246 ARPEGGIOS

247 INTERVALS

248 INTERVALS

249 BALANCE AND INTONATION: DIATONIC HARMONY

250 BALANCE AND INTONATION: MOVING CHORD TONES

251 BALANCE AND INTONATION: LAYERED TUNING

252 BALANCE AND INTONATION: FAMILY BALANCE

253 EXPANDING INTERVALS: DOWNWARD IN PARALLEL OCTAVES

254 EXPANDING INTERVALS: DOWNWARD IN TRIADS

255 EXPANDING INTERVALS: UPWARD IN TRIADS

256 RHYTHM: SIMPLE METER (3/4)

257 RHYTHM: COMPOUND METER (12/8)

258 RHYTHMIC SUBDIVISION

259 CHANGING METER: 4/4 AND 5/8

260 CONCERT F MINOR SCALE AND CHORALE
Chris M. Bernotas (ASCAP)

261 CHORALE
Chris M. Bernotas (ASCAP)
Menacingly

262 CHORALE
David R. Gillingham
Aggressive and forceful

263 CHORALE
Frédéric Chopin
Arranged by Michael Story (ASCAP)
Andante moderato

264 CHORALE
Jack Stamp
With purpose and resolve

265 CHORALE
Andrew Boysen, Jr.
Dark and dramatic

Concert D♭/C♯ Major

266 PASSING THE TONIC

267 LONG TONES

268 CONCERT D♭/C♯ MAJOR SCALE

269 SCALE PATTERN

270 SCALE PATTERN

271 FLEXIBILITY

272 CHROMATIC FLEXIBILITY

273 ARPEGGIOS

274 INTERVALS

275 BALANCE AND INTONATION: MOVING CHORD TONES

276 BALANCE AND INTONATION: SHIFTING CHORD QUALITIES

277 EXPANDING INTERVALS: DOWNWARD IN PARALLEL OCTAVES

278 EXPANDING INTERVALS: UPWARD IN PARALLEL FIFTHS

279 CONCERT D♭ MAJOR SCALE AND CHORALE

Chris M. Bernotas (ASCAP)

A

B

280 CHORALE

Chris M. Bernotas (ASCAP)

With motion

mf

281 CHORALE

Roland Barrett (ASCAP)

Flowing

Concert B♭ Minor

282 PASSING THE TONIC

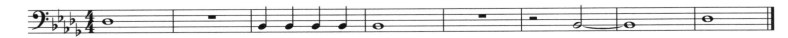

283 CONCERT B♭ NATURAL MINOR SCALE

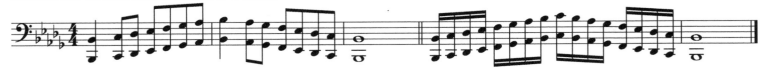

284 CONCERT B♭ HARMONIC AND MELODIC MINOR SCALES

harmonic minor scale   melodic minor scale

285 SCALE PATTERN

286 SCALE PATTERN

287 FLEXIBILITY

288 ARPEGGIOS

289 INTERVALS

290 BALANCE AND INTONATION: LAYERED TUNING

291 BALANCE AND INTONATION: DIATONIC HARMONY

292 EXPANDING INTERVALS: DOWNWARD IN TRIADS

293 EXPANDING INTERVALS: UPWARD IN TRIADS

294 CONCERT B♭ MINOR SCALE AND CHORALE

Chris M. Bernotas (ASCAP)

295 CHORALE

Stephen Melillo (ASCAP)

Rubato, slowly as felt

296 CHORALE

Ralph Ford (ASCAP)

Passionato

Concert C Major

297 **PASSING THE TONIC**

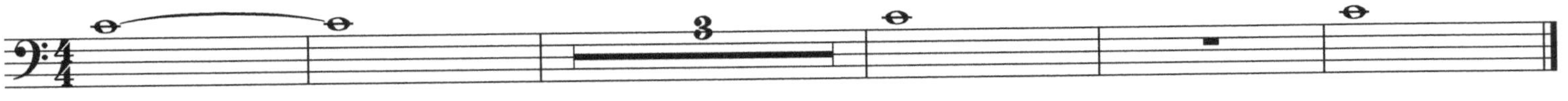

298 **CONCERT C MAJOR SCALE**

299 **SCALE PATTERN**

300 **SCALE PATTERN**

301 **FLEXIBILITY**

302 **ARPEGGIOS**

303 **INTERVALS**

304 BALANCE AND INTONATION: MOVING CHORD TONES

305 BALANCE AND INTONATION: LAYERED TUNING

306 EXPANDING INTERVALS: DOWNWARD IN PARALLEL OCTAVES

307 EXPANDING INTERVALS: UPWARD IN PARALLEL FIFTHS

308 CONCERT C MAJOR SCALE AND CHORALE

Chris M. Bernotas (ASCAP)

309 CHORALE

Chris M. Bernotas (ASCAP)

Flowing

310 CHORALE

Robert Sheldon

Gently

Concert A Minor

311 **PASSING THE TONIC**

312 **CONCERT A NATURAL MINOR SCALE**

313 **CONCERT A HARMONIC AND MELODIC MINOR SCALES**

harmonic minor scale   melodic minor scale

314 **SCALE PATTERN**

315 **SCALE PATTERN**

316 **FLEXIBILITY**

317 **ARPEGGIOS**

318 **INTERVALS**

319 **BALANCE AND INTONATION: MOVING CHORD TONES**

320   BALANCE AND INTONATION: DIATONIC HARMONY

321   EXPANDING INTERVALS: DOWNWARD IN PARALLEL OCTAVES

322   EXPANDING INTERVALS: DOWNWARD IN TRIADS

323   CONCERT A MINOR SCALE AND CHORALE

Chris M. Bernotas (ASCAP)

324   CHORALE

Randall D. Standridge

325   CHORALE: AIR, HWV 467

Georg Fredrich Handel (1685–1759)
Edited and Arranged by Todd Stalter

Majestically
(opt. woodwind and bells 1st time, brass/percussion 2nd time)

Concert G Major

326 PASSING THE TONIC

327 CONCERT G MAJOR SCALE

328 SCALE PATTERN

329 SCALE PATTERN

330 FLEXIBILITY

331 ARPEGGIOS

332 INTERVALS

333 BALANCE AND INTONATION: MOVING CHORD TONES

334 BALANCE AND INTONATION: SHIFTING CHORD QUALITIES

335 EXPANDING INTERVALS: DOWNWARD IN PARALLEL OCTAVES

336 EXPANDING INTERVALS: UPWARD IN PARALLEL FIFTHS

337 CONCERT G MAJOR SCALE AND CHORALE

Chris M. Bernotas (ASCAP)

338 CHORALE

Stephen Melillo (ASCAP)

339 CHORALE

Andrew Boysen, Jr.

Concert E Minor

340 **LONG TONES**

341 **CONCERT E NATURAL MINOR SCALE**

342 **CONCERT E HARMONIC AND MELODIC MINOR SCALES**

343 **SCALE PATTERN**

344 **SCALE PATTERN**

345 **FLEXIBILITY**

346 **ARPEGGIOS**

Concert A Major

355 **CONCERT A MAJOR SCALE AND CHORDS**

356 **SCALE PATTERN**

357 **BALANCE AND INTONATION: MOVING CHORD TONES**

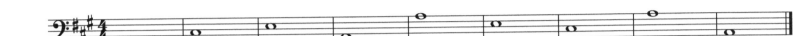

358 **CHORALE**

Chris M. Bernotas (ASCAP)

Concert F♯ Minor

359 **CONCERT F♯ NATURAL MINOR SCALE AND CHORDS**

360 **CONCERT F♯ HARMONIC AND MELODIC MINOR SCALES**

361 **SCALE PATTERN**

362 **BALANCE AND INTONATION: LAYERED TUNING**

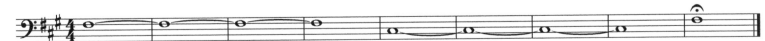

363 **CHORALE**

Chris M. Bernotas (ASCAP)

Concert D Major

364 **CONCERT D MAJOR SCALE AND CHORDS**

365 **SCALE PATTERN**

366 **BALANCE AND INTONATION: MOVING CHORD TONES**

367 **CHORALE**

Chris M. Bernotas (ASCAP)

Concert B Minor

368 **CONCERT B NATURAL MINOR SCALE AND CHORDS**

369 **CONCERT B HARMONIC AND MELODIC MINOR SCALES**

370 **SCALE PATTERN**

371 **BALANCE AND INTONATION: LAYERED TUNING**

372 **CHORALE**

Chris M. Bernotas (ASCAP)

52

Concert B/C♭ Major

373 CONCERT B/C♭ MAJOR SCALE AND CHORDS

374 SCALE PATTERN

375 BALANCE AND INTONATION: PERFECT INTERVALS

376 CHORALE

Chris M. Bernotas (ASCAP)

Concert G♯/A♭ Minor

377 CONCERT G♯/A♭ NATURAL MINOR SCALE AND CHORDS

378 CONCERT G♯/A♭ HARMONIC AND MELODIC MINOR SCALES

379 SCALE PATTERN

380 BALANCE AND INTONATION: MOVING CHORD TONES

381 CHORALE

Chris M. Bernotas (ASCAP)

Concert E Major

382 **CONCERT E MAJOR SCALE AND CHORDS**

383 **SCALE PATTERN**

384 **BALANCE AND INTONATION: LAYERED TUNING**

385 **CHORALE**

Chris M. Bernotas (ASCAP)

Concert C# Minor

386 **CONCERT C# NATURAL MINOR SCALE AND CHORDS**

387 **CONCERT C# HARMONIC AND MELODIC MINOR SCALES**

harmonic minor scale

melodic minor scale

388 **SCALE PATTERN**

389 **BALANCE AND INTONATION: MOVING CHORD TONES**

390 **CHORALE**

Chris M. Bernotas (ASCAP)

Concert F#/G♭ Major

391 CONCERT F#/G♭ MAJOR SCALE AND CHORDS

392 SCALE PATTERN

393 BALANCE AND INTONATION: PERFECT INTERVALS

394 CHORALE

Chris M. Bernotas (ASCAP)

Concert E♭ Minor

395 CONCERT E♭ NATURAL MINOR SCALE AND CHORDS

396 CONCERT E♭ HARMONIC AND MELODIC MINOR SCALES

397 SCALE PATTERN

398 BALANCE AND INTONATION: LAYERED TUNING

399 CHORALE

Chris M. Bernotas (ASCAP)

Bassoon Fingering Chart

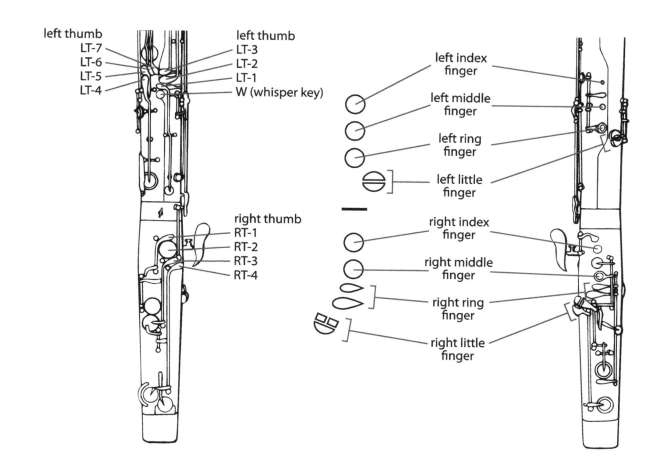

left thumb
- LT-7
- LT-6
- LT-5
- LT-4

left thumb
- LT-3
- LT-2
- LT-1
- W (whisper key)

- left index finger
- left middle finger
- left ring finger
- left little finger

right thumb
- RT-1
- RT-2
- RT-3
- RT-4

- right index finger
- right middle finger
- right ring finger
- right little finger

○ = open
● = pressed down
◐ = half hole covered
LT = left thumb
RT = right thumb

Bassoon players use a technique called flicking, not on any other instrument. This involves the momentary pressing (or "flicking") of the high A, C, or D keys by the left hand thumb at the beginning of certain notes in the middle octave in order to help achieve a better start to the note. Any note that is not responsive or cracks between octaves may benefit from using this technique.

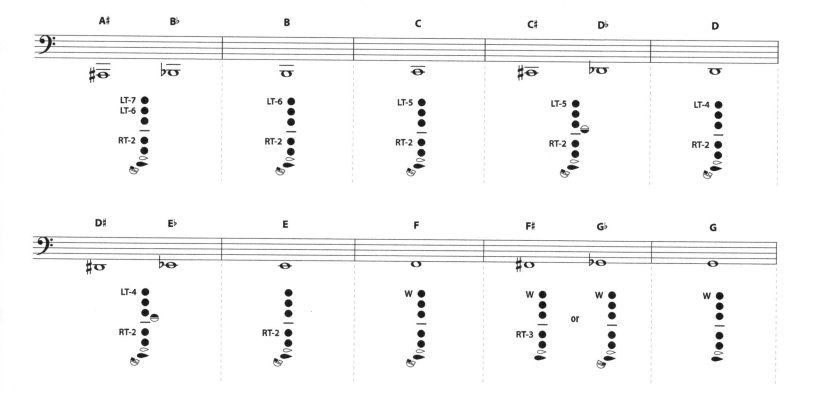

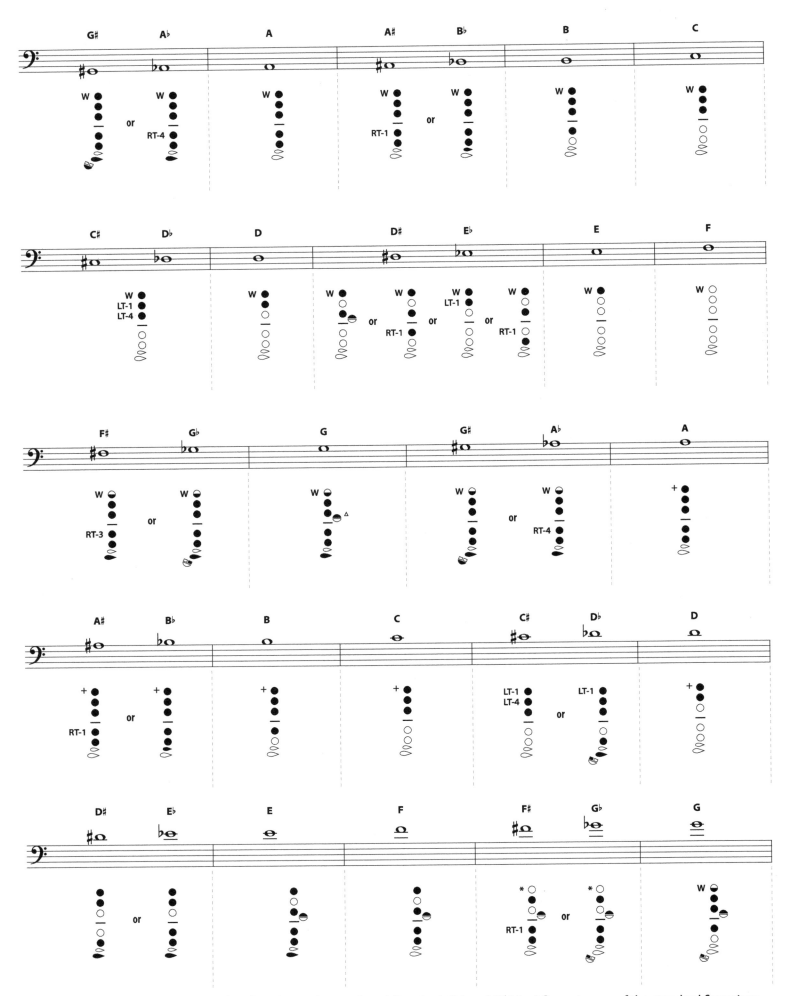

*On some bassoons, high F#/Gb can be played more in tune by adding the left-hand 3rd (ring) finger to one of the standard fingerings.
+The stability of this note can be improved by touching or "flicking" LT-2 or LT-3 at the beginning of the note.
△Either left pinky can be used depending upon the intonation of the instrument.